Facing Midlife

The Bible Reading Fellowship
15 The Chambers, Vineyard
Abingdon OX14 3FE
brf.org.uk

The Bible Reading Fellowship (BRF) is a Registered Charity (233280)

ISBN 978 0 85746 581 8
First published 2017
10 9 8 7 6 5 4 3 2 1 0
All rights reserved

Acknowledgements

Scripture quotations from The Holy Bible, New International Version (Anglicised edition) copyright
© 1979, 1984, 2011 by Biblica. Used by permission of Hodder & Stoughton Publishers, a Hachette UK
company. All rights reserved. 'NIV' is a registered trademark of Biblica. UK trademark number 1448790.

Every effort has been made to trace and contact copyright owners for material used in this resource. We
apologise for any inadvertent omissions or errors, and would ask those concerned to contact us so that
full acknowledgement can be made in the future.

A catalogue record for this book is available from the British Library

Printed and bound by CPI Group (UK) Ltd, Croydon CR0 4YY

Facing Midlife

Tony Horsfall

Introduction

I am passionate about helping people on their journey through midlife because I know that, although it can be a tricky period to navigate well, it also provides a great opportunity for significant spiritual growth.

Over the years that I have been leading retreats and spending time with individuals, I have seen time and again the importance of midlife. Many issues seem to coalesce in our 40s and 50s and it is hard for us to deal with them on our own. That is why people instinctively seek outside help, from wise friends and respected advisors, as well as from books like this one. We have a need to understand, to explore our thoughts and feelings and to talk over what we are experiencing in a safe and accepting context.

I also know from my own experience how crucial midlife can be. For me, it coincided with the decade of my 40s and was a period of inner turmoil. I faced many challenges in my work as a church leader, but also struggled with issues within myself. I sought help, but could find very little. At times, I felt alone and vulnerable. That I got through midlife relatively unscathed is down to the grace of God. I know I could have made some bad choices and easily taken a wrong path.

At the same time, midlife became a significant turning point for me. For most of my adult life I had been engaged in Christian ministry, firstly in mission work overseas and local church ministry, then in a training ministry. My life was full of activity and most of the time I felt exhausted. Something inside me said, 'There must be a better way to live than this.' About that time, I attended my first silent retreat, and it turned me upside down. I discovered the power of stillness and silence, and the joy of a more contemplative approach to life and faith. More significantly, I entered into the reality of my identity as a deeply loved child of God and discovered the joy of intimacy with God.

I was impacted deeply by this and, about two years later, began to sense that God wanted me to take a step of faith and to launch out into a ministry of my own, aiming to help others experience a life of intimacy with God. Since our children had grown up and left home, and we were ready to downsize, we sold our large family home, paid off the mortgage and bought a smaller, more manageable house. This gave me confidence to follow a new calling for the second half of my life.

Fifteen years later, I can only stand amazed at how God has provided for us, opened doors of opportunity and used me to encourage others. I could never have imagined all that he would do in me and through me. The post-midlife years have been the best years of my life. It feels as if everything that came before, while valuable in itself, was a preparation for this period. Even the period of turmoil proved, with hindsight, to have been particularly formative.

That is why I am delighted to write this series of devotions on the midlife journey. My hope is that, as you read these notes on a daily basis, you will have time to ponder and reflect on what the Bible has to say, consider where you are in life, understand what God is doing in you and find a sense of where God may be leading you in the future.

I wish you a safe passage!

Numbering our days

Our days may come to seventy years, or eighty, if our strength endures; yet the best of them are but trouble and sorrow, for they quickly pass, and we fly away. If only we knew the power of your anger! Your wrath is as great as the fear that is your due. Teach us to number our days, that we may gain a heart of wisdom.

Wise people are those who recognise their days are limited. We each have a finite amount of time to live, which means we should value every day as a gift and make the most of the opportunities we are given.

When we are young, and our whole lives lie ahead of us, we think we have all the time in the world and we cannot imagine life ever coming to an end. As we grow older and we recognise how quickly time passes, we begin to appreciate how precious life is. We feel the need to manage our days more carefully.

When does this change in outlook take place? During what we call midlife, a period that begins when we first realise there are probably more days behind us than there are ahead of us. This is a sobering thought that usually occurs when people are in their 40s – which is right on schedule according to the timetable of this psalm. This realisation helps to focus our thinking and invites us to take stock of our lives.

It makes good sense to pause and think about the way we are living and what we might do in the future – to reflect, evaluate and appraise. By the time we have reached our 40s, we will have learned a good many things about ourselves, about God, about other people and about life itself. Things may not have worked out exactly as we thought they would, and we may feel the need to stop and ask ourselves, 'What do I want to do with the rest of my life? Will it be more of the same, or something different?'

Lord, sometimes it feels like I am at a fork in the road, and uncertain which way to take. Guide me, I pray, so I may do your will. Amen

I was young and now I am old

The Lord makes firm the steps of the one who delights in him; though he may stumble, he will not fall, for the Lord upholds him with his hand. I was young and now I am old, yet I have never seen the righteous forsaken or their children begging bread. They are always generous and lend freely; their children will be a blessing.

Midlife is the transition between the first half of life and the second, that movement from when we were considered 'young' to when we begin to be described as 'old'. For most, this is an unwelcome change which may be met with denial and disbelief, or even with a sense of panic. We may try our best to stave off the ageing process: to keep fit, dress fashionably, stay up to date and so on, but that is only to postpone the inevitable. Wise people accept that changes are taking place – physically, psychologically, emotionally, spiritually – and realise they have to adjust accordingly.

The midlife transition may well be spread out over a period of time, even as long as a decade. It does not always involve a crisis, although it may well be a time when we are tested and tried in a number of ways as we adjust to a new reality. For many, the midlife journey is more like a series of bumps in the road, with challenges that we have to negotiate every now and then. These challenges are part of the normal maturation process we go through as human beings, and while they bring with them a certain danger (of making poor choices), they also bring a great opportunity (of making good choices).

From a faith perspective, midlife is often one of our most formative periods when profound changes take place that enable significant spiritual growth. It is not to be feared. Along with the psalmist, we can be sure of God's faithfulness and that, when we entrust our way to him, he will bring us safely through. What may help in this transition is to share the journey with others who have walked the way before – either a mentor, spiritual director or peer group. There is no need to be alone.

Lord, make my steps firm and my pathway straight. Amen

Midlife angst

The words of the Teacher, son of David, king in Jerusalem: 'Meaningless! Meaningless!' says the Teacher. 'Utterly meaningless! Everything is meaningless.' What do people gain from all their labours at which they toil under the sun? Generations come and generations go, but the earth remains forever.

One characteristic of midlife is a certain amount of soul-searching. This may not always plumb the depths of despair as totally as we see in today's reading, but often midlife throws up a degree of *angst*, of wondering if it has all been worthwhile.

Some may look back over their lives with a feeling of satisfaction, having reached their goals and made a success of life so far. Even such people, however, may experience what has been called 'success panic' and wonder if they can sustain their achievement into the future. Others may look back on broken dreams and hopes that have been shattered. Faced with the stark realisation that they may never achieve the ambitions of their youth, they may live with a quiet despair.

In midlife, it is common for deep existential questions to arise within us. We may ask, 'Is that it?' Having worked hard and achieved our goals, we may question if it was worth all the effort and sacrifice. Success does not always bring the fulfilment we expect. We may wonder, 'Is this as good as it gets?' Having lived life to the full, we may be left feeling empty and searching for an inner satisfaction that seems elusive.

We may feel, 'There must be a better way to live than this.' In the first half of life we have often worked hard and long, and we arrive at midlife feeling exhausted and worn-out. The prospect of nothing but more of the same leaves us frustrated and disillusioned.

Such questions are our friends, not our enemies. We should not be afraid of them, for they set us on a journey to find true meaning and purpose, to discover that which makes life worth living. They take us deeper into God, and may lead us to the discovery that he has something better in store for us.

Lord, you know my questions. May they lead me closer to you rather than drive me away. Amen

God knows and understands our struggles

As a father has compassion on his children, so the Lord has compassion on those who fear him; for he knows how we are formed, he remembers that we are dust. The life of mortals is like grass, they flourish like a flower of the field; the wind blows over it and it is gone, and its place remembers it no more.

For those who are believers, the midlife journey is lived out in the context of their relationship with God. While some may begin to question their faith and doubt previously firmly held convictions, others may well discover that their faith finds a much deeper expression than before.

One reassuring truth we can hold on to is that God knows and understands us, and has compassion on us. Although we may be surprised at the turmoil we experience in midlife, God is neither shocked nor troubled by the twists and turns of our human journey. The God who made us understands us better than we understand ourselves, and is actually at work in all that is happening to us.

Midlife can be a time of great disorientation. Someone described it as like losing your way in a dark wood, fearing you may never find the way out again. It can feel like we have lost our bearings, as if the compass we have relied upon is no longer accurate, and we don't know which way to turn. We don't understand ourselves, those around us don't understand us, and we are left adrift and at sea.

If you feel this way, take heart. There is no need to blame yourself for your inner turmoil; it is par for the course when passing through midlife. God has not abandoned you, nor will he ever forsake you. Your heavenly Father is watching over you even as you process so many different emotions and unfamiliar thoughts. He will see you through and you will come out the other side stronger, wiser and more compassionate than ever. What is needed now is to trust, to take the hand of God and know that you are in the grip of his grace.

Father, sometimes I feel lost, confused, lonely and afraid. I believe you are with me though, and will see me safely through. Amen

God's ultimate purpose

And we know that in all things God works for the good of those who love him, who have been called according to his purpose. For those God foreknew he also predestined to be conformed to the image of his Son, that he might be the firstborn among many brothers and sisters.

It is easy in life to make the mistake of thinking that what matters most is *what we do*, when in reality God is more concerned with *who we are*. Indeed, in the first half of life the emphasis is likely to be on building a career, achieving our goals and making our dreams come true. Then, in midlife, we begin to realise that God's agenda for us is somewhat different. He is concerned about who we are becoming and the formation of our character.

The story of Joseph is an example. Sold out of hatred by his brothers to Midianite traders, he found himself transported down to Egypt. There, he was unjustly imprisoned until eventually he was released into Pharaoh's service. God prospered him and he became second only to the king himself in authority. When famine came and his brothers arrived seeking help, Joseph was in a position to help them. Having been humbled by God through his suffering, he was able to forgive them; and having been raised up to prominence by God, he was able to meet their need.

Joseph explained to his brothers: 'Do not be distressed and do not be angry with yourselves for selling me here, because it was to save lives that God sent me ahead of you… It was not you who sent me here, but God… You intended to harm me, but God intended it for good to accomplish what is now being done, the saving of many lives' (Genesis 45:5, 8; 50:20).

God used adversity to shape Joseph's character and to bring him to the place where he could serve God's purpose. Midlife is a time to look back over your life and see how God has been at work in your circumstances, working all things together for your ultimate good.

Lord, as I look back, help me to see your guiding hand in the ups and downs of my life. Amen

Discovering your past

Then you shall declare before the Lord your God: 'My father was a wandering Aramean, and he went down into Egypt with a few people and lived there and became a great nation, powerful and numerous. But the Egyptians ill-treated us and made us suffer, subjecting us to harsh labour. Then we cried out to the Lord, the God of our ancestors, and the Lord heard our voice and saw our misery, toil and oppression. So the Lord brought us out of Egypt with a mighty hand and an outstretched arm, with great terror and with signs and wonders.'

The people of Israel were encouraged to remember their history through story and ritual. The festival of Firstfruits was a reminder to them of their ancient past and of their ancestry that went right back to Abraham.

A characteristic of midlife is to focus on the past, and one of the signs of this is a certain nostalgia for what we have left behind. This can show itself in many ways, from attending school reunions to tracing our ancestors. We may want to revisit the places where we grew up or connect with friends from years gone by. It is as if something inside us wants to find our roots, to know where we came from.

When we were growing up, we couldn't wait to move on – to leave school, enter further education, start a career, get married, move away and so on. We were in such a hurry to enter adult life that we had no time to say goodbye. Now it seems we can only find ourselves by piecing together the past.

This can be especially poignant for those who have been adopted or fostered from an early age. Often, in midlife they experience a powerful urge to find their birth mother or father, to be reunited with siblings and thereby make sense of their early life.

As we discover more about our past, we can better appreciate the factors that have shaped us and made us who we are. We are better placed then to grow in self-awareness and self-understanding, both essential prerequisites for personal growth and transformation.

Lord, thank you that nothing about my past was hidden from you; you have shaped me through it all. Amen

Making peace with the past (1)

Remember, Lord, your great mercy and love, for they are from of old. Do not remember the sins of my youth and my rebellious ways; according to your love remember me, for you, Lord, are good. Good and upright is the Lord; therefore he instructs sinners in his ways. He guides the humble in what is right and teaches them his way.

The backward glance so characteristic of the midlife transition helps us to appraise our life thus far. It is important that we recognise and appreciate what has been good in all that has gone before – what we have achieved, the blessings we have received and the things for which we are grateful. This can be used as the basis for genuine thanksgiving to God. A spirit of gratitude and celebration for what has been will make our transition into the second half of life much easier.

At the same time, we may be aware of our mistakes and failures. We may have a certain amount of regret over things that have happened, and with the perspective of hindsight may wish we had behaved differently or made better choices. However, the past cannot be changed and we must come to an acceptance of the way things are so that we can find peace to move into the future unencumbered with baggage from the past.

Receiving God's forgiveness is the best way to achieve this. God has made provision for this through the death of his Son at Calvary, and when we confess our sins to him we are able to receive his pardon. This forgiveness is freely given and, on the basis that God has forgiven us, we can forgive ourselves as well. We need no longer blame ourselves or carry a burden of guilt and shame. We can know the peace of God.

The recognition that we are not perfect keeps us humble, and having received grace ourselves we are more able to give grace to others. It also places us in a better position spiritually so that we can be more responsive to God's leading in the future.

Lord, I thank you that you are both good and upright. Imperfect as I am, please lead me in your ways, especially as I pass through midlife. Amen

Making peace with the past (2)

When Joseph's brothers saw that their father was dead, they said, 'What if Joseph holds a grudge against us and pays us back for all the wrongs we did to him?' So they sent word to Joseph, saying, 'Your father left these instructions before he died: "This is what you are to say to Joseph: I ask you to forgive your brothers the sins and the wrongs they committed in treating you so badly." Now please forgive the sins of the servants of the God of your father.' When their message came to him, Joseph wept.

We have already alluded to the story of Joseph and his brothers, and the great injustice he suffered at their hands. Although God used his suffering to accomplish a good purpose, there still remained the question of forgiveness and the possibility that they might be reconciled.

The reason that many people do not like to think about the past is because it has been painful. They have been hurt by others, in some cases treated unfairly or unjustly, perhaps even mistreated or abused. A common way of dealing with inner pain is to stuff it down inside us and forget all about it – except that the hurt never really goes away. We can live for many years like this, but again it is a feature of midlife that old wounds tend to resurface and demand our attention.

Now, we are on extremely sensitive ground here, and often it requires very skilled help (counsellors, psychotherapists, etc.) to unpack safely the most severe buried pain. We should only attempt to do this if such help is available. For most of us, thankfully, our pain is not so severe. Following simple biblical guidelines will help us find release so we can move forward.

First, we must receive God's forgiveness for ourselves. Then, with God's help, we must forgive those who have hurt us, refusing to hold on to any bitterness or grudges. Finally – and this is never easy, and not always possible – we can seek to be reconciled to those who hurt us.

Forgiveness is a process that takes time and courage, and must never be rushed. It is made possible only by God's grace.

Lord, heal my hurt and help me become willing to forgive. Amen

Choosing the better part

But Martha was distracted by all the preparations that had to be made. She came to him and asked, 'Lord, don't you care that my sister has left me to do the work by myself? Tell her to help me!' 'Martha, Martha,' the Lord answered, 'you are worried and upset about many things, but few things are needed – or indeed only one. Mary has chosen what is better, and it will not be taken away from her.'

If the first phase of midlife involves coming to terms with the past, then the second involves becoming aware of the changes that are taking place within us in the present. This interior work is often slow and requires us to have great patience with ourselves, and also with God.

Many people in midlife feel the pull towards interiority – the desire to develop their inner life and to get to know themselves, and God, more deeply. This movement is initiated within us by the Holy Spirit, and the longing we feel is created by him as he draws us towards greater intimacy with the Father.

The first half of life tends to be lived mostly in the outer world of activity, often at great pace and with high energy. There is much that we want to achieve, much that we should be doing, much that we desire to experience. This leaves little time for stillness or reflection and can leave our souls threadbare and dehydrated. Like Martha, we are distracted by our own busyness.

Not surprisingly, people often reach midlife feeling exhausted and overwhelmed, even on the edge of burnout. It comes as good news to realise there is a better way to live, one that involves us living from the inside out. Like Mary, we can discover the joy of sitting at the feet of Jesus, hearing what he has to say and then living our lives accordingly. By incorporating stillness and silence into our lives, we discover that our souls are refreshed, our joy is restored and our lives can still be effective and fruitful. This is the better way to live.

Lord, help me not to be distracted by busyness. Show me how to live my life from the place of intimacy with you. Amen

Finding your true identity

See what great love the Father has lavished on us, that we should be called children of God! And that is what we are! The reason the world does not know us is that it did not know him. Dear friends, now we are children of God, and what we will be has not yet been made known. But we know that when Christ appears, we shall be like him, for we shall see him as he is.

The movement towards the inner life as the basis for, and strength behind, the outer life is a significant feature of spiritual growth in our midlife years. The discovery that we are called to intimacy with God and that we can enjoy a deep and satisfying relationship with him is inseparably linked to the realisation of our true identity: that we are God's deeply loved children.

The natural human tendency is to create an identity for ourselves, and we may do this in any number of ways. Most commonly we base our identity on what we do (occupation), what we accomplish (achievements), what we have (possessions) and what other people think of us (reputation). All of these add to our sense of well-being and self-worth, but the reality is that building an identity on such external markers is like building on shifting sand. None of these are permanent; all of them can be lost. Should that happen, our world will come tumbling down.

Our true and unshakeable identity is to be found only in God, and he declares us to be his deeply loved children. Such an identity can never be lost because it depends upon God's unchanging love for us, not on our performance or achievement. Here is solid ground on which to build our sense of worth and value. Who am I? I am God's beloved child!

Knowing you are loved unconditionally gives you confidence to draw near to God and develop a relationship with him. It also allows you to be honest before him, and, knowing you are loved and accepted as you are, to be open to the change and transformation that is essential to spiritual growth.

Lord, help me to see myself as you see me, and to live as your beloved child. Amen

The great cover-up

Then the eyes of both of them were opened, and they realised they were naked; so they sewed fig leaves together and made coverings for themselves. Then the man and his wife heard the sound of the Lord God as he was walking in the garden in the cool of the day, and they hid from the Lord God among the trees of the garden. But the Lord God called to the man, 'Where are you?'

We have described already the movement we experience in midlife towards interiority, recognising the importance of the inner life and finding our true identity as God's beloved child. Alongside this comes a second movement: the desire for authenticity.

The story of Adam and Eve in the garden tells how sin came into the world and disrupted their relationship with God. Previously, they had enjoyed meeting God in the cool of the day, but now they are afraid of him and want to avoid his presence. Their strategy is twofold: to cover themselves with leaves because they feel ashamed, and to hide among the trees because they feel guilty.

This disconnection from God is something that characterises each of us and it leads us to adopt similar strategies as we seek to get by in the world without God. Shame is the negative feeling we have about who we are, and guilt is the negative feeling about what we have done. These two troublesome emotions cause us to cover up and hide our true selves, both from God (which is impossible) and others (which is not as easy as we think). This leads to the creation of a 'false' self, an identity we fashion for ourselves but is not who we really are.

The false self is not evil or bad – it is just not authentic. We wrap it round ourselves like a set of clothes, protecting our hidden self from others while projecting into the world the self we want them to see. In the first half of life, the false self may help us get by, but in midlife we often experience a longing to shed our pretence and start living authentically – in other words, to be who I really am, the person God intended me to be.

Lord, give me courage to grow into my true self. Amen

True to myself

Saul said to David, 'Go, and the Lord be with you.' Then Saul dressed David in his own tunic. He put a coat of armour on him and a bronze helmet on his head. David fastened on his sword over the tunic and tried walking around, because he was not used to them. 'I cannot go in these,' he said to Saul, 'because I am not used to them.' So he took them off. Then he took his staff in his hand, chose five smooth stones from the stream, put them in the pouch of his shepherd's bag and, with his sling in his hand, approached the Philistine.

Saul was concerned for David's safety as he prepared to face Goliath, and offered his armour to the young boy out of a genuine concern for his welfare, but it was not what he needed. Saul's armour was made for Saul, and it did not fit David, so it would have been a hindrance in his fight with Goliath. Wisely, David refused to be weighed down and chose to face his enemy with what he already had – his sling, some stones and his faith in God.

Some people reach midlife weighed down by the expectations of others. We can live for many years trying to fulfil such expectations from parents, teachers, religious leaders, even spouses. We struggle to do so because such pressure forces us into a mould that does not fit who we really are. This is another way in which the false self is created. We conform ourselves to the expectations of others, and we become what they want us to be, losing our true self in the process.

Midlife seems to be the time when we feel the need to break this mould and be true to our self. This can be extremely difficult to do because it may mean disappointing others, but it is essential for our spiritual growth. The point is this: we do not need to wear another person's armour, or try to be what we are not. We are free to be the person God made us to be, at home in our unique self and trusting God. That is enough.

Lord, help me become the person you intended me to be, free of pretence. Amen

What the true self looks like

Therefore, as God's chosen people, holy and dearly loved, clothe yourselves with compassion, kindness, humility, gentleness and patience. Bear with each other and forgive one another if any of you has a grievance against someone. Forgive as the Lord forgave you. And over all these virtues put on love, which binds them all together in perfect unity.

Transformation is like a change of wardrobe – we take off one set of clothes and replace them with another. Paul had already reminded the Colossian believers of what the old clothes looked like and now describes the new ones, itemising for them the characteristics the Holy Spirit would form within them.

The true self is who you are as God created you and who you are in Christ. Stepping into your true identity releases you to be authentic and to live without pretence or having to cover up. It also gives you permission to be who you really are, with your unique gifting and personality, without trying to be like anyone else.

This is not a licence to live selfishly or sinfully, but rather a call to become more like Jesus. Midlife does not give us a mandate to act irresponsibly or simply for personal gratification or fulfilment. The true self is based upon who we are in God and therefore operates within a moral framework that is based on the commandments and expressed by loving others. Any choices we make should reflect these values. Your true self will always be the best version of yourself.

When we live from our false self, we are never quite being real. It feels forced, a little unnatural, and it requires effort. When we live from our true self, it is just the opposite – it feels easy, quite natural, and takes less effort because we are being genuine. Most importantly, we are freed to become more like Jesus than ever before. Not that this can be accomplished simply by willpower or self-determination. It requires a deep work of the Holy Spirit and a willingness on our part to choose to walk in obedience and love.

Lord, I so desire to live this new life and to become more like Jesus. Enable me by the power of your Sprit I pray. Amen

Understanding the shadow

We know that the law is spiritual; but I am unspiritual, sold as a slave to sin. I do not understand what I do. For what I want to do I do not do, but what I hate I do. And if I do what I do not want to do, I agree that the law is good. As it is, it is no longer I myself who do it, but it is sin living in me. For I know that good itself does not dwell in me, that is, in my sinful nature. For I have the desire to do what is good, but I cannot carry it out. For I do not do the good I want to do, but the evil I do not want to do – this I keep on doing.

I believe that Paul's words here are autobiographical – he is describing his own experience as a believer, not writing hypothetically about someone else. His struggle reflects the battle with sin that, if we are honest, we all face.

Midlife calls for a healthy introspection and honest self-examination. This is not navel-gazing or self-preoccupation, but is indicative of a necessary self-awareness that is critical to personal maturity. If we are to change, we must get to know ourselves and be aware of our weakness and potential to self-implode.

All of us have what we might call a 'shadow side', a part of our self that is unrecognised, suppressed or even denied. It contains aspects of our personality we choose not to acknowledge or show to others, but which remain dormant within us. However, when we are under stress, suffering exhaustion, feeling ill or for some reason less in control of our behaviour, the shadow side can erupt on to the surface of life with great psychological force. It can cause us to say and do unhelpful things, taking both ourselves and others by surprise.

This hidden, immature self is, of course, part of who we are which we must acknowledge and bring to God so that we can change. Paul's answer was to be filled daily with the Holy Spirit, as he so wonderfully describes in Romans 8. It is our answer as well.

Lord, help me to know myself. Daily fill me with your Spirit. Amen

Known yet loved by God

You have searched me, Lord, and you know me. You know when I sit and when I rise; you perceive my thoughts from afar. You discern my going out and my lying down; you are familiar with all my ways. Before a word is on my tongue you, Lord, know it completely. You hem me in behind and before, and you lay your hand upon me. Such knowledge is too wonderful for me, too lofty for me to attain.

Psalm 139 is the most personal of all David's psalms and describes the deep interaction between the man and his God. He is deeply aware that nothing about him is hidden from God, nor is there any place where he can avoid the divine presence. Whatever he does, God sees it; wherever he goes, God is already there. He appears both disturbed and reassured by this understanding.

Self-knowledge is essential for spiritual growth. In midlife, God allows our shadow side to be revealed, giving us insight about who we really are. We are stripped of all pretence as to our own goodness in order that we may depend more fully on the righteousness that is ours in Christ (Romans 3:20–24; Philippians 3:8–9). This may be wounding to our pride but it is essential to our spiritual well-being.

David's psalm reminds us that we are known completely by God, and yet loved and accepted just the same. This awareness, that I am loved *as I am*, is the basis of all future transformation since it liberates me to acknowledge my sin and failure, and thus be forgiven and healed.

Sometimes it is our failure that opens the door to God's grace. We fall into grace when we admit our sin and weakness and discover that, as the hymn writer Charles Wesley (1707–1788) said, in Christ there is 'grace to cover all my sin'. The experience of grace warms our hearts and kindles the flame of devotion within us. Realising we are known through and through, and yet are still loved without reservation, motivates us to love God in return and offer ourselves to him to do his will.

Lord, may I have the courage to open myself up to you completely, knowing I am loved as I am. Change me from within. Amen

Faith in turmoil

Now Thomas (also known as Didymus), one of the Twelve, was not with the disciples when Jesus came. So the other disciples told him, 'We have seen the Lord!' But he said to them, 'Unless I see the nail marks in his hands and put my finger where the nails were, and put my hand into his side, I will not believe.'

Thomas will forever be associated with the adjective 'doubting' because he demanded further proof that Jesus had indeed risen from the dead. His absence from the upper room meant he missed seeing the risen Jesus, and he felt he needed his own tangible confirmation before he could believe.

Midlife can be a time when people of previously strong faith find themselves doubting things they were once sure about. Those whose faith has been handed down to them and uncritically accepted may well find they need to examine again the basis of their faith and why it is they believe. This is, of course, a healthy thing, and part of the natural way in which faith develops and matures.

Others, even those who have been active in leadership roles and vibrant in their faith expression may suddenly find themselves experiencing a crisis of faith. They may have been hurt and let down by fellow believers or feel bored by church life. They may be disappointed with God when prayers are not answered and ventures of faith apparently fail. They may have questions about the veracity of the Bible or queries about certain doctrines. They may wonder if God has abandoned them or even if he cares at all.

Such turmoil is common in midlife. In our earlier years, our ideas about God have probably been clear and certain, and our faith largely untested. By midlife, we will have faced circumstances that have challenged our assumptions about God and faith and will lead us to a period of review. We should not fear such reappraisal because, even though it may take time, it can bring us to a deeper and more robust faith. Talking things through with a trusted adviser may be helpful.

Remember that the Lord who was patient with Thomas will be patient with you.

Lord, I believe; help my unbelief. Amen

Midlife marriage

Love is patient, love is kind. It does not envy, it does not boast, it is not proud. It does not dishonour others, it is not self-seeking, it is not easily angered, it keeps no record of wrongs. Love does not delight in evil but rejoices with the truth. It always protects, always trusts, always hopes, always perseveres. Love never fails.

Midlife can be a time of great personal turmoil and this inevitably affects our relationships with others, especially those closest to us. They will feel the intensity of our struggle and have to deal with our instability. Marriage in particular comes under great strain in midlife.

Married people in midlife often find themselves 'squeezed' between caring for elderly parents on one hand and their children on the other. For some, there is the pain of an 'empty nest'. There may be challenges at work: carrying greater responsibility, facing competition from younger colleagues, finding themselves overlooked for promotion or feeling the threat of redundancy. They may have less time for each other and feel jaded in their relationship. Several of these factors coming together can create the perfect storm resulting in strained relationships, the possibility of an affair and, sadly for some, divorce.

It is important that couples work at their relationship, recognising the importance of keeping love alive. Having quality time together, listening to one another, talking honestly and openly, and resolving any conflict wisely will help. They will need lots of patience, mutual forgiveness and good grace. Some will find a Marriage Enrichment course helpful; others may benefit from seeing a marriage counsellor. It is important to stay committed to the vows we made earlier in life, and to keep believing that with God's help we will find our way to a deeper and more satisfying relationship.

Those whose marriages do not survive the storms of midlife need not despair. There is healing after the tsunami of grief, and there is hope of rebuilding life again from the ashes. If we give ourselves time and remain positive, we can recover our self-worth and start again. It will require a great deal of courage and spiritual strength, but with God's grace it is possible.

Lord, help me to keep loving no matter what happens. Amen

Single in midlife

I would like you to be free from concern. An unmarried man is concerned about the Lord's affairs – how he can please the Lord. But a married man is concerned about the affairs of this world – how he can please his wife – and his interests are divided. An unmarried woman or virgin is concerned about the Lord's affairs. Her aim is to be devoted to the Lord in both body and spirit. But a married woman is concerned about the affairs of this world – how she can please her husband. I am saying this for your own good, not to restrict you, but that you may live in a right way in undivided devotion to the Lord.

Single people in midlife are often glad not to face the same pressures as their married friends, but they have significant challenges of their own, and often have to face them alone. They enjoy the freedom to make their own choices and have greater flexibility to make changes in their lives, enabling them to follow God's leading with less disruption. If they have already come to terms with singleness, they will be able to devote themselves to their career and to serving God without distraction. These are very positive factors in midlife.

At the same time, even for the most dedicated people, emotional pain may never be far away. Many, while enjoying the benefits of being single, would still love to have a life partner and will still feel the ache of loneliness. Others may be hit in midlife with the realisation that they may never marry or have children or grandchildren. While their married friends can usually mark their lives by their children's milestones – starting school, passing exams, going to university, getting married, having their own children – single people can feel like they are missing out. They can feel vulnerable when making major decisions and may be fearful of what the future holds.

The church needs to provide a welcoming community for single people, helping them to make friendships and overcome loneliness. Single people themselves can invest time in quality relationships, show hospitality to others, enjoy other people's children and anchor themselves firmly in God.

Lord, may I serve you with undivided devotion whatever my situation. Amen

Made by God for his purpose

The word of the Lord came to me, saying, 'Before I formed you in the womb I knew you, before you were born I set you apart; I appointed you as a prophet to the nations.' 'Alas, Sovereign Lord,' I said, 'I do not know how to speak; I am too young.' But the Lord said to me, 'Do not say, "I am too young." You must go to everyone I send you to and say whatever I command you. Do not be afraid of them, for I am with you and will rescue you,' declares the Lord.

As we come to the later stages of midlife, it is as if the mist clears and we can see what it has all been about. Much of the inner work will have been done and we are ready now to enter into the second half of life and embrace the opportunity it offers.

Vocation is a term usually reserved for those who feel called to a particular religious work (being a priest or missionary), but that definition is too narrow. Vocation reminds us that God has a calling for each one of us, in whatever sphere of life we feel most at home, and he created us with that purpose in mind. This calling can be expressed in any number of ways, but it will always flow out of who we are as unique individuals and will be an expression of our love for God and desire to serve others.

As we seek to discern what this will look like we can ask ourselves three questions: (1) Who am I as a person? (2) What are my gifts? and (3) What is my passion, the thing I most love to do? It is in the coming together of these factors – our identity, gifting and passion – that we can identify the will of God for us.

This may mean we continue to do what we did before, but with greater conviction and purpose. It may mean that we take a step of faith and do something we have never done before. Either way, we can look forward to being more fruitful and effective than ever.

Lord, give me understanding of your will for me at this stage of my life. Amen

Taking steps of faith

By faith Abraham, when called to go to a place he would later receive as his inheritance, obeyed and went, even though he did not know where he was going. By faith he made his home in the promised land like a stranger in a foreign country; he lived in tents, as did Isaac and Jacob, who were heirs with him of the same promise. For he was looking forward to the city with foundations, whose architect and builder is God.

When we speak about finding our vocation, we are not suggesting that the first half of life has been wasted or merely incidental to the real work. No, the first half has been worthwhile in itself, and may also have been lived vocationally, but now we enter into our most fruitful years by building on all that has gone before. As Richard Rohr has said in *Falling Upwards* (SPCK, 2012), in the first half we are building a container, and in the second half we are putting in the contents.

In the second half, we look for those opportunities where who we are and what we do come together. When this happens, we are at our most effective and we work most efficiently, so we have great joy and satisfaction. That does not mean that what God calls us to will be easy or straightforward, but hopefully we will have a sense that this is the purpose for which we were made, and that it fits.

Making changes at this stage often requires a step of faith, leaving behind the familiar and secure in order to step into something new and different. Faith is a dynamic within us that moves us, like it did Abraham, to do great things for God.

This is where the adventure of faith comes in and it is what makes the midlife transition so exciting. We have before us the possibility of discovering God's will for the next phase of our life and activating the dreams that God has placed in our hearts. Moving forward, though, will require a certain boldness and courage, but when we respond we may find that in the second half we make possibly our greatest contribution.

Lord, I pray that fear will not hold me back from doing your will. Amen

Generativity

Since my youth, God, you have taught me, and to this day I declare your marvellous deeds. Even when I am old and grey, do not forsake me, my God, till I declare your power to the next generation, your mighty acts to all who are to come.

'Generativity' is a term used to describe the desire to establish and guide the next generation, to pass on what we have learned to benefit others and to make a lasting difference with our lives. It is the opposite of 'stagnation' whereby we become locked into ourselves and our own needs, without caring for others. Midlife reflects the struggle between these two tendencies. Those who make the best transition, and whose lives are the most fulfilled, are those who choose the way of generativity.

In the first half of life, it is natural to be concerned for our own growth and development, to want to be successful and achieve our goals. In the second half, as we become more secure in ourselves, we can be less self-centred and more other-centred. Knowing our true identity as God's beloved children frees us from a preoccupation with self and releases us into helping others reach their potential.

A parent has by definition the capacity to be generative, to give life to others and to nurture growth. Part of our vocation is to become fathers and mothers in God. This is not about making people dependent on us, but helping them reach their full potential. The struggles of our midlife transition are what make this kind of investment in others possible.

Generativity can be expressed in any number of creative ways – spending quality time with younger family members, sharing our stories of God's faithfulness and power, being there to support younger leaders, providing a listening ear, getting involved in causes of social justice and so on.

We should never make the mistake of thinking we have nothing to give. Everyone has something to pass on to the next generation and, if we are willing to be used by God, he will show us what we have to offer, and the best way to do so.

Lord, make my life a blessing to others. May I freely share what you have so freely given. Amen

Legacy

You then, my son, be strong in the grace that is in Christ Jesus. And the things you have heard me say in the presence of many witnesses entrust to reliable people who will also be qualified to teach others.

The apostle Paul gave much of his time and energy to developing those around him, in particular the young man Timothy. Having met him on his third missionary journey, Paul identified his potential and took him under his wing so that he became like a son in the faith (Acts 16:1–3). He not only taught Timothy the faith but set an example for him, helped him grow into maturity and eventually become leader of the church at Ephesus. Paul wrote two epistles (1 and 2 Timothy) to further encourage his protégé.

Generativity includes the idea of leaving a legacy, of passing on something of value to the next generation. We often think of legacy in terms of the money or property that is bequeathed to someone, but legacy can also be about influence, skills and knowledge. In midlife, we are not only thinking about the contribution we will make ourselves in the future but also how we can invest ourselves in the next generation by passing on the baton of leadership.

One of the best ways to do this is by mentoring others, working with them on a one-to-one basis (or small group) to help and support them according to our expertise and experience. This may involve coaching them in particular skills, offering encouragement and advice when needed, or opening doors of opportunity. It might be done informally or in a more structured and intentional way. Mentoring is a ministry that seems especially suited to those who have passed through midlife.

An important aspect of mentoring is offering the time and space to listen to others. Listening is a skill in its own right, and since most of us are not good at it, it is worth finding some appropriate training so we can do it well. Listening is the greatest gift we can offer to another person, and sharing the journey with them will be one of the best contributions we ever make.

Lord, help me to invest in others for the sake of your kingdom. Amen

priority

Learning to abide

Remain in me, as I also remain in you. No branch can bear fruit by itself; it must remain in the vine. Neither can you bear fruit unless you remain in me. I am the vine; you are the branches. If you remain in me and I in you, you will bear much fruit; apart from me you can do nothing.

Having discovered our God-given purpose for the second half of life, and realised the importance of investing in others and leaving a legacy, we may throw ourselves into the task with renewed energy and vigour, not realising that we cannot live in later life as we did when we were younger. Our energy decreases as we get older. If we are to avoid the danger of burnout and live in a way that is sustainable, we will need to operate differently than before.

In the first half of life, we have often lived our lives *for* God, doing all that we can to please him and to do his will. The danger is that we do this in our natural strength and energy, which is never sufficient and which leaves us exhausted. In midlife, we seek a better way to live, where we learn to work *with* God, which is totally different. Here we see the Christian life as a partnership, where God is the senior partner who initiates and directs while we respond to his leading. This way of living and working is more sustainable and more effective, and is built around the practice of abiding in Christ.

Jesus teaches his disciples through the picture of the vine how to live in a way that will be fruitful. A branch cannot produce fruit by itself; it must be connected to the vine. When the branch remains in the vine, it receives life from the vine and naturally bears much fruit; if it becomes detached, it ceases to be fruitful.

The implication is clear: we will only be fruitful if we stay in a close relationship with Jesus, drawing our strength and life from him. This is why it is important to nurture our inner life and live in dependency on him.

Lord, teach me to abide in you and to work in partnership with you. Amen

Midlife parables

The kingdom of heaven is like treasure hidden in a field. When a man found it, he hid it again, and then in his joy went and sold all he had and bought that field. Again, the kingdom of heaven is like a merchant looking for fine pearls. When he found one of great value, he went away and sold everything he had and bought it.

Jesus was a master storyteller. His parables often hit the mark with disarming simplicity. Here are two stories about discipleship: giving all we have to find the most important thing in life. True disciples set the kingdom of God as their priority. For them, knowing God is their greatest joy and what they value most of all.

The midlife journey is not an easy one. It requires us to be honest with ourselves, to face up to our need for personal transformation and to allow God to work deeply within us. It requires us to make radical choices and significant adjustments to the way we live, and to take courageous steps of obedience and faith as we move into the future God has for us. What this does is seek out and expose our true values. What do we really desire? What is most important to us? How far will we go in our discipleship?

These two men were both willing to sell everything because they had seen something better – the one treasure hidden in a field, the other a pearl of great value. Only when we have seen the wonderful possibilities that the midlife transition holds for us will we be willing to pay the price that is involved, that of radical openness to God. If we can hold before us the vision of coming through midlife changed and transformed, with a clearer sense of purpose and the potential to make our most significant contribution yet, then we will find the motivation to keep going when the way is hard.

Not all are willing to follow this way. For some, the price is too high. They opt out, settling for a comfortable existence or choosing their own path. Midlife is a crossroads. Which way will you choose?

Lord, give me grace to follow and make the right choices. Amen

Shaped by the potter

This is the word that came to Jeremiah from the Lord: 'Go down to the potter's house, and there I will give you my message.' So I went down to the potter's house, and I saw him working at the wheel. But the pot he was shaping from the clay was marred in his hands; so the potter formed it into another pot, shaping it as seemed best to him. Then the word of the Lord came to me. He said, 'Can I not do with you, Israel, as this potter does?' declares the Lord. 'Like clay in the hand of the potter, so are you in my hand, Israel.'

Jeremiah's visit to the potter's house became for him a moment of spiritual revelation. As he watched the skilful hands of the potter, he saw a picture of God, the divine potter, who works in our lives to make us the people he wants us to be.

I love the term 'spiritual formation' because it describes this very process. Just as the potter knows what kind of vessel he is making, so does God, and he works in us with that in mind. He is not simply concerned about what we *do*, but with who we *are*, and just as importantly, who we are *becoming*. Character matters to God and his desire is that the life of Jesus should be formed within us (Romans 8:28–29; Galatians 4:19). It is not just about serving God, but being made like him.

It also suggests that a degree of pressure is necessary for this to happen. Something is being formed, fashioned, shaped; this does not happen by accident or by chance, but by the application of a degree of force. This requires the potter to have skilful and sensitive hands to apply just the right amount of pressure. How reassuring as we pass through midlife! God is behind much of our midlife turmoil, applying the sort of pressure that brings change, yet never more than we can bear.

The clay for its part must be soft and malleable in the potter's hand, not resisting his shaping, but responding to his hand. Likewise, we must cooperate with God's working in our lives.

Lord, I gladly place myself in the Potter's skilful hands. Amen

Wisdom for the journey

Listen, my son, accept what I say, and the years of your life will be many. I instruct you in the way of wisdom and lead you along straight paths. When you walk, your steps will not be hampered; when you run, you will not stumble. Hold on to instruction, do not let it go; guard it well, for it is your life.

I find it helpful to think of life as a journey, indeed as a pilgrimage, because it is a journey made with God. Midlife is a crucial part of this journey, linking as it does the first half of life with the second. It can be rightly described as a dangerous journey because, as we have seen, there are many challenges along the way, and there is always the possibility of losing our way. On the other hand, if we follow the wisdom of God and walk in his way then we will find a glorious future opening up before us where the second half surpasses whatever has gone before.

How then do we keep on track? Here are five simple guidelines for making a good transition.

1 Understand the process. Midlife is a normal and natural part of human growth and spiritual development, and I have tried to outline my understanding of what it involves. Understanding this process equips you to cope with the turmoil and make sense of what is happening.
2 Recognise the hand of God. God is watching over you and is in control of all your circumstances. He wants you to make a safe passage and his grace is available every step of the way.
3 Take time to step back. It is worth making space to reflect on your life and, perhaps with the help of another individual, to consider what God is doing in you and where he may be leading you.
4 Keep track of what is happening. Writing a journal will be helpful, and reviewing what you have written from time to time will give perspective.
5 Trust in God. Believe that God is with you, even in darkness or uncertainty, and that his purpose for you will come to pass.

Lord, I want to make this journey with you. Help me to walk in your way. Amen

Transforming
lives and communities

Christian growth and understanding of the Bible

Resourcing individuals, groups and leaders in churches for their own spiritual journey and for their ministry

Church outreach in the local community

Offering three programmes that churches are embracing to great effect as they seek to engage with their local communities and transform lives

Teaching Christianity in primary schools

Working with children and teachers to explore Christianity creatively and confidently

Children's and family ministry

Working with churches and families to explore Christianity creatively and bring the Bible alive

Visit **brf.org.uk** for more information on BRF's work
Review this book on Twitter using **#BRFconnect**

brf.org.uk

The Bible Reading Fellowship (BRF) is a Registered Charity (No. 233280)